LISTEN WITH THE HEART

$\mathcal{L}$ISTEN WITH THE $\mathcal{H}$EART

SACRED MOMENTS
IN EVERYDAY LIFE

JOAN CHITTISTER, OSB

SHEED & WARD
*Lanham * Chicago * New York * Oxford*

Published by Sheed & Ward
An Imprint of Rowman & Littlefield Publishers, Inc.

A Member of the Rowman & Littlefield Publishing Group
4501 Forbes Boulevard, Suite 200, Lanham, MD 20706
www.rowmanlittlefield.com

PO Box 317
Oxford
OX2 9RU, UK

Library of Congress Cataloging-in-Publication Data

Chittister, Joan.
    Listen with the heart : sacred moments in everyday
  life / Joan Chittister.
       p.   cm.
    ISBN 1-58051-139-2 (pbk. : alk. paper)
    1. Meditations.   2. Christian life—Catholic authors.   3. Catholic
  Church—Prayer-books and devotions—English.   I. Title.
  BX2182.3.C48 2003
  242—dc21   2003000839

Printed in the United States of America

⊗™ The paper used in this publication meets the minimum requirements
of American National Standard for Information Sciences—Permanence
of Paper for Printed Library Materials, ANSI/NISO Z39.48-1992.

To Sister Maurus Allen, OSB,
model of monasticism for me, guide to my growing—
with gratitude and affection

CONTENTS

INTRODUCTION

There are moments in life that are either too numbing or too exhilarating, too sad or too exciting for us to absorb. Death and marriage, loss and victory, deep sadness and great joy can all overwhelm us. We are struck dumb before them all. We find ourselves looking for ways to express what we're feeling and can't. We don't know what to say and we can't think of what to do. We live in a state of emotional suspension, aware that we are in a holy moment and unsure how to mark it so.

There are times that are too emotionally demanding or, on the other hand, too beautifully commonplace to comprehend—the birth of the baby; the return of a sister, long gone but always missed; a visit to the site of one of life's great beginnings each cry out to be treated reverently. But with what? And how? Beauty in the midst of ugliness can leave us speechless; the most meaningful of routines can leave us untouched. The very routinization of the meaningful things in life—the quick kiss goodbye in the morning, the family meal at night, the first day in the new house, the last day of class—can doom us to sleepwalk through life, vaguely aware that we are in the presence of the profound but unable to make it recognizable, let alone significant, for others.

In times like these, we all need to be carried beyond the immediacy of the situation to realize the elements of the sacred that underlie all the facets of life. Rituals—those formal patterns of behavior that mark the crossover moments of time and make them sacred—jolt the soul and wake us up to life. Funeral liturgies tell us how to get through grief. Birthday parties tell us how to attend to growth and age. Christmas teaches us surprise and sharing.

But, by and large, modern life does not lend itself to mindfulness. We are a fast-moving, quick-changing society. We live in a culture of planned obsolescence. Nothing much is made to last anymore. Stability is not what this culture is about. We don't get into the habit of repeating things because either we or our neighbors are not here from one year to the next to share those events again together. Even family traditions began to break down in contemporary culture when we began to lose touch over the miles with the generations who were the carriers of our past. We have lost a sense of the importance of those holy echoes in life that take us back to our roots, make us remember our formative moments, carry us beyond the routines of life.

This book is an attempt to enrich the present dearth of tradition in a highly mobile society with an ancient, family-centered spirituality, known now as Benedictine monasticism. Its meaning for people today is only beginning to be recognized but it may well be, for a culture in flux, the missing link to our loss of roots. The Rule of Benedict, written over 1m500 years ago, is based on the passage of time and the importance of every hour, every action in life. It is grounded in mindfulness, awareness, and a sense of the sanctity of the present moment. This book is rooted in that kind of consciousness. Its purpose is to heighten our sensitivities to the point that there is no such thing as a moment without meaning for us.

Monastic life is not an excursion into either great asceticism or an ecstatic prayer life. Monastic life is the sacrament of the ordinary. It is the ordinary lived in consciousness of the Ultimate. The monastic drinks life dry. Everything in the monastery has meaning. We walk into chapel in a certain way for a certain reason. We pray certain things at certain times over and over again so that we never forget that this particular event in life is gift and that all of life has lessons to teach us in the midst of the most mundane of days. Monastic life is consciously divided into differing segments of time so that time is never taken for granted, never ignored, never to be seen as useless or wasted or dull.

Ritual becomes a way of life for us. We construct ceremonies to mark the moments that people come to the monastery—and to bless them on their way if and when they go. We create ceremonies to mark the taking on of ministries. We eat traditional menus for traditional occasions. We drink wine on feast days and dance around the Paschal Candle on Easter. We still go in procession to bless the Christmas cribs in the monastery, singing songs that have been in the community for years, poor as they are theologically, bad as they are musically. And we bless one another commonly, as well. We use candles to mark the movement of the seasons. We bow at prayer, prostrate during Lent, and sing the Suscipe, the formal song of self-surrender, at times of profession and jubilee. We pray around the bed of a dying sister for hours. We gather in prayer to share memories of her when she dies, both laughing and crying at her leaving. These things are our way of saying that all of life is holy. All of life is blessing. All of life is rich with possibility and surprise. It is the ordinary things in life lived extraordinarily well that make life real. This book is grouped around themes—prayer, naming, music, meals, death, waiting, darkness, and community, among others—to enable a reader to identify the kind of life event or activity that might best mark the various moments in life. Most of all, they are presented in such a way that each element can be reflected on individually and separately or as a total topic from multiple perspectives. The book can be used privately or discussed in a group.

Listen with the Heart is about the import and meaning of rituals that are common to monasticism and, in many ways, to us all. They are an invitation to families and parishes, to individuals and groups everywhere to make the mundane meaningful again.

BLESSING

Numbers 6:24

May God bless you and keep you; may God's face shine upon you and be gracious to you; may God look upon you kindly, and give you peace.

The scene had become a relatively common one. The community—younger sisters and old—stood with hands outstretched over the sister kneeling in the center of the chapel as they had so many times before. She was going into a war zone in Central America to accompany dislocated peasants on the long walk through occupied territory back to their lands. The community was blessing her. Suddenly I began to think of all the other blessings we do just as regularly, just as solemnly.

On the feast of the Epiphany, the community goes from area to area in the monastery blessing the house, blessing each room as they go.

After prayer every morning and evening, the prioress blesses the community.

Every year, in recognition of the fact that the Rule of Benedict calls for the blessing of those who are called to community service, we gather as a community 1,500 years later for the ceremony of the Blessing of Ministries.

We have blessed our new Garden of Memories that enshrines for us the memory of our dead, our new inner-city program facilities and our three hermitages in the woods.

As long as I can remember, we have blessed the Christmas tree each year. And we bless the women as they enter our community and those who are breathing their last in it.

And now the community has begun the practice of holding prayer vigils at sites of recent homicides in our city to bless that violent place with new peace.

In fact, we bless everything in sight. Why? Because blessings are the life breath of those who believe in the sacredness of space and place, all things and life.

Blessing is an ancient custom which, perhaps, could profit a people who live under schedules that leave us breathless and unsatisfied, who are surrounded by technology that promises more than it gives, who find themselves in such unrelenting pursuit of the good life that it so easily blurs the good in the present life.

Blessings are the visible demonstration of faith in the goodness of the God whose blessings are often invisible.

God bless you.

❧

To bless a thing is to remind ourselves that this very object is one of God's gifts given to bring us to wholeness of life. Once we understand that, we will also realize that it is the way we respond to things in life that makes us holy. Then nothing is for nothing in our lives.

❧

To bless someone is to recognize as sacred what God recognizes as sacred, an awareness too little called to mind in a world where the self is made to be always more important than the other.

❧

Blessing is a way of acknowledging that the God who created us goes on lavishing life upon us all our days.

❧

In ancient Israel, a gift was understood to be a blessing made visible. To give a birthday present, for example, was a way of demonstrating that God's favor for us never ended. It wasn't consumerism gone mad; it wasn't social protocol gone plastic. It was simply living proof that life is genuinely full of God's blessings. How sad to lose that meaning.

❧

"Every day is a god," Annie Dillard wrote, "each day is a god, and holiness holds forth in time." Learning to see that holiness is everywhere we are, is the reason we bless both the obvious and the hidden goods of life.

❧

Here's the difference between mental stability and mental imbalance: The mentally healthy person is able to see the possible blessing in every event in life.

❧

Everything in life is a potential blessing. It only depends on how we view it and what we do with it.

❧

Don't be surprised when what you think is a blessing turns out to be sour. We so often confuse the holy with what is only seductive.

❧

If you can't find your blessings where you are, don't look for them elsewhere. As Hildegard of Bingen, Benedictine abbess of the twelfth century said, "Holy persons draw to themselves all that is earthly." It's what we're given to work with in life that are our real blessings.

❧

What we bless we declare to be part of what it takes to makes us holy: houses, people, death, prayer, relationships.

❧

In order to begin to see the blessings in life, we have to get over cursing everything around us.

❧

There is such a thing as a negative blessing. What we do not question, for instance, we bless. As the Roman Tacitus wrote on the subject of the assassination of the Emperor Galba: "A shocking crime was committed on the unscrupulous initiative of a few individuals, with the blessing of more, and amid the passive acquiescence of all." The point is clear: What we see as sacred is one thing. What we do not call attention to as evil is another. Both are blessings of a sort. The only question is which of them we practice.

❧

Perhaps if we did more blessing of our children and less brutalizing of them, we would have a more peaceful, more gentle generation of children.

❧

In Jewish tradition, the practice of blessing the other was not reserved to the priests. Parents blessed their children, rulers blessed their people, even Balaam, the outsider, is ordered by Yahweh to bless Israel. We are required, obviously, to be open to the blessings of the other everywhere.

❧

In Israel, every greeting was a form of blessing. Conversations opened, in other words, by asking God to do good to the person to be addressed. Think about it: If we did that yet today, we would call down good on every person we met before we said another word. It must be pretty difficult to hate someone after that.

❧

Why do we bless things? Madeleine L'Engle says it well: "There is nothing so secular that it cannot be sacred, and that is one of the deepest messages of the Incarnation." Everything God made is good. To bless it is simply to acknowledge that.

❧

The ancients never doubted that a blessing, once pronounced, released a force which was beyond the control of the one who said it. It had a power of its own. Now modern psychology tells us that the words we say to another shape their psyche and mark them for life. Clearly, blessings work on levels we never think about. So why did we drop them?

❧

We are all a means of blessing for one another. You have to want to be a blessing, of course. And who knows? Maybe the problem is not that we don't see the blessings around us. It may be that we fail to see ourselves as blessings. And so we aren't.

❧

The worthier the person who blesses, the Israelites taught, the more effective the blessing. The lesson was clear: God pours out blessings on us especially through those who are themselves most good. It's just another way of saying that we need to watch the company we keep.

❧

We are often blessed in ways we can't imagine. Instead of getting what we want, we get what we need. The problem is that it takes longer to understand that what we didn't want is precisely what, in the end, was best for us.

❧

Biblical blessings express God's generosity, favor and unshakable love. They call on God, who is the source of all life, to give fullness of life now as always. Blessings are, in other words, a pretty good bet.

❧

Blessing is one of the ways that God makes the presence of God known here and now.

❧

Blessings are the way we celebrate the everyday goodness of our lives. By reminding ourselves always of the bounty in which we ourselves are immersed, we save ourselves from the burden of coveting the lives of others.

❧

The practice of blessing the good things of life turns our hearts and our personalities from sour to sweet. When we learn to see the value of what we have, we stop fretting about what we don't have. And we're nicer about it, too.

❧

What if, for just one day, we blessed our animals for their companionship, the children of the neighborhood for the ring of laughter they bring to our streets, the people who serve us and our friends in their struggles? What if someone blessed us with courage for the day and strength for the journey? What if we realized our own role in the calling down of the blessings of God on the things of the earth, the places we live and the work we do? What if blessing became a commonplace again? Then, how would we possibly ever despair of God's presence?

❧

Blessing is not magic and it is not superstition. It is recognition of the fact that God's wonders are worked for us every day. If we really believe that life is sacred and good and full of the touch of God, isn't it time to start saying so again?

❧

Don't say that blessing is a priestly activity and has nothing to do with you. To the ancient Jews, the "priestly blessing of Aaron" was a strictly liturgical act. It was on the blessing of one another that the people lived. It's time to begin the cycle of blessing that makes every person and place and thing special, noticed, celebrated.

❧

The truth is that each of us is necessarily either blessing or curse to the people around us. How much better—both for them and for ourselves—to be a conscious blessing to another than a burden on the way.

❦

Christina Baldwin wrote, "Ritual is the way we carry the presence of the sacred. Ritual is the spark that must not go out." The right and obligation to bless the world around us is simply another way of making the presence of God present to those who advert only to God's absence.

❦

"To renew ties with the past need not always be daydreaming," Simeon Strunsky wrote. "It may be tapping old sources of strength for new tasks." In a world in which we cannot have everything, whatever our efforts, we may never have had need of blessings more. Blessings make us realize what we do have and allow us to mark them for the world to see—and learn.

❦

The seeker whispered, "God, speak to me." And a meadowlark sang. But the seeker did not hear. So the seeker yelled, "God, speak to me!" And the thunder rolled across the sky. But the seeker did not listen. The seeker looked around and said, "God, let me see you." And a star shone brightly. But the seeker did not notice. And the seeker shouted, "God, show me a miracle." And a life was born. But the seeker did not know. So the seeker cried out in despair, "Touch me, God, and let me know that you are here!" Whereupon God reached down and touched the seeker. But the seeker brushed the butterfly away and walked on. Moral: Don't miss out on a blessing because it isn't packaged the way you expect.

LIGHT

Ephesians 5:8

For once you were darkness,
but now in God you are light.

It was the year 2000. I was in a Benedictine monastery in Kenya to give a workshop on the Rule of Benedict. The house was amazingly modern, built in large part with money from Germany, and meant to last. It had a large novitiate wing, marble floors, hot and cold running water, a clinic for the poor and—for six hours every day—no electricity. The only problem was that no one ever knew which six hours the electricity would go off. It could be midday. Sometimes it was in the middle of the night. Often there was no light for Morning Praise at 6:00 a.m. or for Evening Praise at 6:30 p.m. At those times, each sister lit a small candle at her pew. It made me think.

On the Sabbath vigil, our own monastery prayer opens in the darkness of a densely quiet chapel, not because we have no electricity but because we are in need of a spiritual reminder. The community sits in the shadows of the night and waits.

Then, suddenly, quietly, unexpectedly, the acolyte comes silently down the shrouded center aisle that leads to the altar, holding high and straight a candle with its tiny flickering flame. Like centuries of Jewish congregations before us, we stand to bless the Light. Like the moment of creation, the new week begins with a promise of life and growth and insight and the presence of the God who is Light in the darkness and Life in the chaos that is in all our lives.

The liturgical use of light, the reminder of the God who is Energy and Life, is a clear one in our monastery yet. Every Advent we watch together as each week another candle points to the coming of the Light that is Christ. On Christmas Eve we bless the lighting of the Christmas tree that is ever green and always a sign of eternal life. Every Holy Saturday we light the lanterns in the chapel hall designed to lead us to the new light of Easter. Every night of our lives the monastery bell tower is flooded in light, a reminder of the

Light that brings life and so makes such a lifestyle of reflection and contemplation both logical and necessary.

Light is clearly the oldest symbol in the Judeo-Christian tradition. The lighting of the Sabbath candles, long before the coming of Christianity, symbolized the presence of the God who is Light. To the rabbis, the light of the candle was at the same time always new, always changing and always the same. It was the ultimate symbol of the God who, in creating humankind out of the substance of Godness, was nevertheless not diminished.

To Christians, light was a sign of new life in Jesus.

And so, we don't use light bulbs or flashlights in chapels, even when the electricity goes out. Even in a technological age. We use candles to this day, the reminder that God is Light, that we are part of the everlasting flame of life, that darknesses everywhere are expelled by the tiniest pinpoints of light. If we will only light them.

❧

Liturgical light is the reminder to us always that no darkness, either around us or within us, is too deep to expel if we try hard enough to bring even the smallest glimmer of hope. The problem is that we are often far too easily convinced that what we are facing is impossible when in reality it is simply difficult.

❧

Never accept as darkness anything that, with a little effort—a slight change of mind, a touch of humor—can become light. Or as Loretta LaRoche puts it, "Optimists live longer. Pessimists are more accurate, but optimists live longer."

❧

Never assume that you can always tell the difference between darkness and light. Some of the most penetrating insights we ever experience come out of the deepest darkness.

❧

Darkness is the place where the tiniest sliver of light means the most. The smallest act of concern can bring lightness of heart to the one whose soul is blanketed in darkness.

❧

Light doesn't show us anything new. It only enables us to see what has always been there.

❧

It's when we face reality head-on that life finally becomes possible, if not exciting. "Light is the first of painters," Ralph Waldo Emerson wrote. "There is no object so foul that intense light will not make it beautiful." What we are willing to deal with well will teach us important things about life, about ourselves.

❧

Always remember that there's a difference between light and heat. Most disagreements, unfortunately, descend to heat, to argumentative differences, when only light—only clarity, insight, and openness to the other—can really resolve the issue.

❧

"God's first creature," Francis Bacon wrote, "was light." God left us in light. Don't you wonder why it is that we so often choose darkness instead?

❧

Sir Muhammad Iqbal makes us pause. He wrote, "Thou didst create the night, but I made the lamp. Thou didst create clay, but I made the cup. Thou didst create the deserts, mountains and forests, I produced the orchards, gardens and groves. It is I who made the glass out of stone, and it is I who turn a poison into an antidote." The point is clear: God gave us the ability to turn the dark spots in life into light. So, why don't we?

❧

There are two kinds of people: those who spread light and those who spread darkness everywhere they go. Determining into which category we ourselves fall can change the course of life, ours and that of people around us, as well.

❧

"Only that day dawns," Henry David Thoreau wrote, "to which we are awake." Translation: If you can't shape your soul to see the possible good in a thing, it won't be there no matter how clear it is to everyone else.

❧

When we bring light into a room, we bring the energy of God into life. "God is light," scripture tells us. So, if we are sincerely seeking God, it's imperative that we position our souls in the light, even when the light of new truth is difficult for us to bear.

❧

We can't take light for granted. Sometimes we are most in darkness at exactly those moments when we are sure that we are most in the light.

❧

Edna St. Vincent Millay wrote: *My candle burns at both ends; / It will not last the night; / But ah, my foes, and oh, my friends / It gives a lovely light.* Pity the life that has nothing for which burning the candle at both ends is worth it. That is, indeed, a very dark life.

❧

The excitement of life lies in always pursuing the light. It winds through darkness and ends in the clear. "Light is meaningful only in relation to darkness," Louis Aragon wrote, "and truth presupposes error. It is these mingled opposites which people our life, which make it pungent, intoxicating."

❧

We do not live in the light at all times. Waiting for the light is part of the process of learning to appreciate it.

❧

There is no amount of darkness that can extinguish the inner light. The important thing is not to spend our lives trying to control the environment around us. The task is to control the environment within us.

❧

To go through life "catastrophizing" everything is to put out the light. Everything in life is not a catastrophe. Most of it is simply normal.

❧

Loretta LaRoche says that 75 percent of daily conversation is negative. We complain about the weather, the traffic, the schedule and sleep! So, she's printed a bumper sticker that says "Stop Global Whining." Join.

❧

We feel the way we think. It takes more energy to "awfulize" a thing than it does to deal with it.

❧

Grieshog, Gaelic speakers tell us, is the process of burying warm coals in ashes at night in order to preserve the fire for the cold morning to come. Instead of cleaning out the cold hearth, people preserved yesterday's glowing coals under beds of ash overnight in order to have fast-starting new fire the next day. It is a holy process, this preservation of purpose, of warmth and light in darkness.

❧

The Irish have another custom associated with *grieshog.* Besides burying the last hot ember of the day in cold coals in order to start the next day's peat fire quickly, the Irish preserve the fire from home to home as well. When a young person marries or when the family moves, they take a hot coal from the first hearth to start the first fire in the new one. The Irish know that no fire lasts forever; the new light has to come from somewhere. The light that has shown us the way this far must not be dimmed.

❧

No one is willing to wait for anything anymore. We have little tolerance, little respect for in-between times. But it may be precisely the in-between times in life that enable us to appreciate both darkness and light in equal measure.

꙳

There's no life that is all light or all darkness. It is learning from both that makes us human, that makes us real.

꙳

"Light," the poet John Ruskin wrote, "is God's eldest daughter." Light is God's sign of creation. Without light nothing grows. But letting new light shine on old ideas is one of the hardest things we ever do, it seems. Instead, we cling to ideas grown dim and call ourselves holy for refusing to change. What an insult to the God of light that is.

꙳

"Goodness is uneventful," David Grayson writes. "It does not flash, it glows." It gives light. It shows the way through dark times. It quietly, steadily leads us beyond the glamour and glitter of life to the home of the heart.

꙳

The Baal Shem Tov said, "The world is full of radiant, wonderful, and elevating secrets, and it is only the small hand held up before our eyes which prevents us from seeing light." Each of us shapes our own darkness by what we refuse to look at, refuse to see, refuse to hold up to the light.

꙳

A Sufi scratching through dust on the road quickly attracted a crowd of onlookers. "Sufi, what are you doing?" the people asked. "I lost my treasure and I'm searching for it," the Sufi answered. So, one by one for hours and hours the people passing by dropped to their knees to sift through the dirt and dig in the ditches. Finally, exhausted by the heat of the day and the fruitlessness of the task, a searcher sighed, "Sufi, are you sure you lost your treasure here?" The Sufi said, "Oh, no, I didn't lose my treasure here. I lost it over there on the other side of the mountain." The tired searchers were shocked. "If you know that you lost your treasure over there," they demanded to know, "Why are you searching for it here?" And the Sufi said, "Because there's more light here." Ask yourself whether you are looking for your own treasure where it is dark or where it is light. Don't take the question for granted.

FASTING

Joel 2:12

Yet even now, says God, return to me with all your heart, with fasting . . . rend your hearts and not your clothing.

Lent settles in over the monastery like a cool, gray mist. Life seems to slow a bit. The liturgies quiet and so does the house. The community gathers in small groups to discuss readings together. There is a stripping away of extras at the community table. Silence, reading and fasting—ancient Lenten monastic practices—become a cocoon in which a sharpened spiritual consciousness, usually submerged in the noise and indulgence and the routinization of the essentials, finds the space to emerge anew. It's a special time. Not punitive, not dour, not grim. It's a time when all the seeds of life come to green in the soul again. I remember the Lent when, after years of those simple monastic practices, the linkages all became startlingly clear.

The deep drums beat with every silent step we took. We'd come, I knew, only about two miles of what they told us was at least a seven-mile route. I'm not a walker. I thought it would never end. In one part of the city the rain beat down. By the time we got through the other part, the sun had melted all the energy I had.

It was Good Friday. As a tangible response to the Lenten readings we had done on the perils of nuclearism, the community had decided to walk the Stations of the Cross publicly this year to draw attention to the fact that a nuclear budget, nuclear weapons and a nuclear mentality stood to crucify contemporary Christianity itself.

When I finally sighted the bell tower of the monastery seven miles out of the center of the city from which the silent walk had begun, I felt a wave of sheer relief. Soon we would be able to sit down. Soon we'd have the nice warm lunch together that would wash some of the weariness away and give us the stamina we'd need for the rest of the *Triduum*: its liturgies, its conferences, our guests.

The morning had begun with *Tenebrae*, that long excursion into sorrowful psalmody and messianic promises. After six hours of praying and walking and silence, I was, I admit, looking forward to the lunch that would precede the Veneration of the Cross that followed it.

So, I remember with particular significance the awareness that came with the realization that the only things on the steam table that day were vegetable soup and crackers and apples. Walk or no walk, the community was fasting. There was nothing "symbolic" about the gesture. We were hungry but we were not going to eat. We were very tired but we were not going to relax together at table. We all had stories about things we'd seen, felt and heard on the walk that we were not going to tell.

I remember something else as well. I remember the sense of deep spiritual consciousness that filled that silent dining room and my own tired self as we processed into chapel that afternoon after six straight weeks of quieting, of shared spiritual reading and of fasting. We had clearly been filled with something far more substantial than food, far more intimate than talk, far more meaningful than rituals done by rote. Lent was not dead time. Lent was the swelling up again of a whole new life that had, under the weight of dailiness, gone dull.

❧

A Lenten regimen of silence, fasting and reading is not meant to dampen life. On the contrary, they are all meant to focus the soul. They sharpen consciousness and give us the opportunity to examine the real hungers, the internal noise, the dulled sense of meaning that sap a life of energy and purpose.

❧

Fasting is an ancient spiritual practice that has lost most of its meaning in modern times. It has been taken over by dieting gurus, health buffs and physical fitness experts. So now in this culture we have bodies that are specimens of good health and souls adrift in search of meaning.

❧

To think of Lent as dismal, as forbidding, as bleak is to fail to realize that part of life's disappointment comes from requiring it to be forever ecstatic, always easy, increasingly exciting. We must make room for seriousness of soul or we can end up with no soul whatsoever.

❧

Fasting does not deprive us of anything. It gives us the opportunity to hold life in perspective, to enjoy it more, to taste the more subtle flavors.

❧

"Silence," Jane Wheelwright wrote, "is another form of sound." Silence is the sound that introduces us to ourselves: to what we're really thinking, to what we're really feeling, to what we really fear. Out of those sounds comes the resurrection of the self.

❧

Sometime during Lent give yourself the gift of silence. Spend one day without turning on the radio, without looking at TV, without making telephone calls. Just bask in the silence, write down what you hear inside yourself or, at the end of the day, tell someone you love what you learned about yourself that day.

❧

God, the Book of Kings says, was not in the whirlwind. God was in the whisper. Silence is where we go to hear the deep, clear voice of God within us. Silence is what gets our attention.

❧

The Internet banner that runs across the top of the *New York Times* says "Indulge." And that may be exactly the problem. Indulgence has become our national passion. We have become so satiated with life that it has lost its flavor. If you really want to enjoy something, give it up for awhile.

❧

Fasting reminds us that we are totally dependent on God. When we fast from something we put ourselves into a state of readiness to grow from whatever it is in life that faces us.

❧

The Rule of Benedict, the oldest continuous monastic rule in the Western world, does not ask for stringent penances during Lent. Benedict asks that we "withdraw some food and add some reading." The relationship is clear: Lent is the time for filling ourselves with ideas that will nourish the soul in the way that nothing else can.

❧

Everyone needs ideas to live by when our reasons for living become unclear. Then silence and reading become the only real mainstays we have to the discovery of the self and the Way.

❧

Ideas change us. In calling for more reading and more silence as basic Lenten practices, Benedict is, then, clearly calling for change, not invariability. The spiritual life is a process of growth, not a checklist of religious activities.

❧

The whole notion that the spiritual life is some kind of constant that can be easily achieved and faithfully kept is a sign of spiritual immaturity. Either we change the way we look at life and God as we grow or we shrivel into some kind of religious cutouts left over from the era before us.

❧

"Nothing so much enhances a good as to make sacrifices for it," the philosopher George Santayana wrote. When we want something badly enough, we pay the price of getting it. Lent is the opportunity to pay the price of getting to know ourselves—our struggles and our limitations—a little better.

❧

We cover up the really important things of life with glut, with racket, with social convention. Fasting and silence and reading are antidotes to the swamping of the self in the flotsam of life.

❧

"I am not now/That which I have been," the poet Byron wrote. The truth is that we change from stage to stage, from year to year, from time to time. Life requires that we stay in touch with ourselves before we lose ourselves. Lent is meant to be the moment of personal rediscovery, the moment we go down into the center of the self to see what remains there, what's missing there, what's in embryo there.

❧

Beware the neurosis of sacrifice, the need to give ourselves away to others so that we can avoid responsibility for what becomes of ourselves. As Carol Pearson put it, "It is one thing to sacrifice briefly one's sleep to comfort a child with a bad dream; it is quite another for a mother to sacrifice her whole career for a child. It is one thing for a father to sacrifice his desire to go fishing today because he needs to go to work to feed the family; it is quite another to work for forty years at a job he hates. . . . Often such massive sacrifice, if not a result of cowardice, comes from an inability to discriminate between giving that is necessary and life-giving and giving that brings death to the martyr and hence to those around him or her."

❧

Lent is the time to escape from the prison of the superficial.

❧

Excessive penance, a hallmark of negative spirituality, makes God some kind of ghoul who delights in seeing the glories of life rejected, destroyed and diminished.

❧

Lent is always a call to conversion. The problem is that we must remember that conversion is not a call to be something other than what we are. Conversion is a call to become more of what we are really meant to be.

❧

Early Israel did not fast simply to atone for sin. They also fasted in preparation for any great undertaking. Lent is the great preparation for life. We fast to restore the spiritual life to its rightful place in consciousness.

❧

Fasting is a prayer. It says, "I trust you, God, to send me what I need in life."

❧

When silence is sullen, it is a sin against society. When silence is reflective, it is an act of creation of the self because out of it comes newness of soul.

❧

Every year during Lent the community fills box upon box with things that the sisters have collected during the year but want to give to the poor. It is a kind of "fasting" from things. If we do not indulge in the superfluities of life, others may have the necessities.

❧

Fasting leads to almsgiving, reading leads to growth and silence leads to change. A Lent of fasting, silence and reading is not the death of the self; it is the springtime of the self.

❧

Jesus was criticized, remember, for not fasting as serious and genuine religious types were expected to do. Instead he ate with those with whom "nice" people, good people, would not think of being seen. When it comes down to it, giving up your reputation for the sake of the outcasts in your crowd is so much harder than giving up chocolate, isn't it?

❧

Early Christians, influenced by the Greek respect for physical vigor, began to see fasting—in addition to the Hebrew expression of supplication, mourning, repentance and spiritual preparation—as a way to discipline the body. But that's the easy part and, too often, the exaggerated part. Spiritual athletes are easy to come by; spiritual people—the kind who grow in compassion and courage—are harder to find.

❧

You don't have to make useless promises at the beginning of Lent. Every day give up one small thing which is within your reach and that you really want. Then, when you need it most, you will have developed the self-control and endurance it takes to sustain a person in hard times.

❧

The purpose of fasting is always, first and foremost, sharing. Augustine wrote in Sermon 208 that "fasting was merely avarice"—a storing up for oneself—"unless one gave away what one would have eaten." So much for "gaining merit."

❧

I gave up coffee creamer for Lent one year. By the end of the tenth day I began to love black coffee. That's the year I learned that it isn't giving things up that matters. It's what you become because of giving it up that counts. Me? I became aware that only internal change really counts.

❧

And now for the big one: Read one new spiritual book this Lent and copy out three ideas in it that you need to think about—because they intrigue you, because they confuse you, or because they encourage you.

PRAYER

Psalm 51:15

*O God open my lips and my mouth
will declare your praise.*

It happened the very day I entered the monastery. First they dressed us in black woolen hose, black shoes, a long black dress, a short black cape and a limp black net veil. Then they walked us, in order of our birthdays, our hands folded piously under our capes, down the long narrow hallway to the monastery refectory where the community waited dinner in silence to pray a first psalm with its newest, youngest members. It was a solemn procession indeed for a group of high-spirited teenage girls. The youngest of the group, I found myself at the very end of the parade.

I remember the scene as if it were yesterday. Light danced through door transoms along the way and cast the shadows of the seven of us, bobbing and weaving silently, along the corridor ceiling toward the stained glass doors at the end of the hall. Then, instead of praying or meditating or reflecting about whatever it is people should be praying about on such a solemn occasion, I remember looking up at the shadows on the wall above us and saying to myself, "I am going to be following this crowd around for the rest of my life."

It's a long time now since the incident happened but I still laugh as I finish telling the story. It is, after all, a clearly inappropriate ending for it, isn't it? What I was thinking at the time, it seemed for years, was obviously wrong. That's what made it funny. In retrospect, however, I can now see that there may have been more insight, more truth, more depth in the observation than I could ever then have dreamed.

I learned later that the walking together into a waiting community was, as a matter of fact, the very embodiment of a communal spirituality, the very bedrock of community prayer. We would, indeed, spend the rest of our lives praying, reflecting and developing together a philosophy and attitude of life formed through the unremitting filter of the psalms. And we would do it at the same time and in the same way during the same regular daily hours of community prayer for the rest of our lives.

I can't help but wonder what would happen to the society around us if we all stopped regularly together to seek the God who is ceaselessly seeking us.

Benedictine liturgical life is daily, regular, constant and communal when the rest of life is chaotic, confused, fragmented and far too involved in lesser things to make time to pray. It is Benedictine prayer, unrelenting in its dailiness, embedded in community, rich with liturgical tradition and aware of the world, that keeps us in touch with the God who illumines us whatever our mundane lives, whatever our daily darknesses.

❧

Benedictine prayer has two basic characteristics. First, it is based on the psalms, the very prayers that formed Jesus himself. And second, it is unceasingly regular, an early answer to the injunction of Jesus to "pray always" as well as a Christian response to the Roman changing of the guard in honor of the Emperor-god. Those two elements, taken together, are dangerously life-changing. They shape attitudes and they make a public declaration of the presence of God in life.

❧

Prayer is the natural response of people who know their place in the universe. It is not designed to be a psychological comfort zone though, surely, comfort it must. Most of all, it is an act of awareness of God and, sitting there in the midst of a praying community, awareness of the rest of the world, as well.

❧

Morning, afternoon and evening—morning, afternoon and evening every day of our Benedictine lives—we present ourselves before the face of God and beg for the insight and the courage it will take to go the next step. Interestingly enough, we didn't make up the prayer style. It had been the tradition of the church, of the synagogue, from the very earliest of times. It remembers God at rising, it gives ourselves over to God at night and it marks the segments of the day, however harried, however dull. So what ever happened to that kind of recollection?

❧

Prayer is what forms us in the presence of God. To fail to do it formally and regularly is to barter the only relationship in life that is guaranteed.

❧

Prayer is more than an exercise. "Pray inwardly," the mystic Julian of Norwich teaches, "even if you do not enjoy it. It does good, though you feel nothing. Yes, even though you think you are doing nothing." The fact is that prayer changes us eventually—if, of course, we pray for what God wants rather than simply for what we want.

❧

We do not pray in order to control God. We pray in order to become new within ourselves, to see differently, to see right.

❧

Prayer is not a pious gesture; it is a response to the One whose heart beats with ours. It is the constant recollection of the living God.

❧

When prayer is regular, we stand the chance of becoming what we pray.

❧

Prayer is not something that happens simply with the uttering of formulas. Real prayer engages us wholly—our minds, our bodies and our hearts. It must be done reflectively and continuously.

❧

If we pray consciously, we will someday become an unconscious prayer.

❧

Real prayer is not a recitation of rote exercises. It is reflection, openness, acceptance and exploration. We consider the meaning of the words we're using, we struggle over the implications of them, we accept the call we hear in them, we ask ourselves what they mean to the way we are living in the world around us, we remember that life is as divine as it is human.

❧

Madame Chiang Kai-shek put it this way: "One cannot expect to be conscious of God's presence when one has only a bowing acquaintance with Him." Not only does God get to know us in prayer but we get to know God, too.

❧

Praying when we do not feel like praying is exactly when we are most vulnerable to the activity of God within us. Which is why we stop in the very middle of other activities to pray together. Then we surrender to what God is trying to say to us here and now rather than to what we are trying to say to God. "Prayer," the French proverb says, "is a cry of hope."

❧

One scripture read every morning and remembered, wrestled with, at regular intervals throughout the day for every day of our lives is more than enough to stretch us beyond ourselves until, finally, finally we have indeed "put on the mind of Christ" and come to the fullness of life.

❧

We don't pray because we're good and holy. We pray because God attracts us and only because God is attracting us. Prayer is our response to the urges of the God within. "Prayer is not asking," Gandhi said, "it is a longing of the soul."

❧

Why do we pray regularly? Because we are never without a need for God—even when we realize it least. Regular prayer reminds us of our real poverty especially when things seem so good for us, especially when we are most likely to think that our life is in our own hands. Or, as the Chinese put it, "In good times we forget to burn incense; in hard times we embrace the Buddha's feet."

❧

Why do we pray the psalms? Because the psalms are the cry of the poor. The psalms keep us tied to the world around us, to what it means to be part of the human community, to the awareness that prayer is not for its own sake only.

❧

Prayer is not an escape into spiritual narcissism. It is an attempt to put on the mind of God, to see the world as God sees the world, to respond to the needs around us as God responds to ours.

❧

If we are too busy to take time for prayerful reflection every day, we are too busy to be human, too busy to be good, too busy to grow, too busy to be peaceful.

❧

In its early stages, prayer is words. In its later stages, prayer is silence. But in every stage, prayer is reflection that must be fed by the words and internalized in the reflections.

❧

Prayer is the wail of the soul to become what we are really meant to be.

❧

In prayer all our smallnesses drop away and we become one with the One.

❧

Daily prayer and immersion in the scriptures bore into the center of the soul until the distance between Galilee and me is no farther away than my next action.

❧

Merton taught us that "Pure love and prayer are learned in the hour when prayer has become impossible and your heart has turned to stone." Prayer, in other words, is not a nest we make in which to hide from the pain of being human. Real prayer comes out of the searing, draining depths of it.

❧

In my monastery we often sing our prayers. Song is that sound which blends best with the sounds of the universe. It is the highest, purest form of thought.

❧

Prayer, rooted in the psalms and scriptures, takes us out of ourselves to form in us a larger vision of life than we ourselves can ever dredge up out of our own lives alone. It plunges us into the feelings and forces of the entire cosmos and shapes us into something bigger than our own small selves.

❧

God does not commonly come to us in prayer in words that match our own. God comes in insights and understandings and feelings that must be carefully culled.

❧

To pray is to go down into a deep well where the sound of the voice of God echoes in the darkness.

※

Prayer gives us the rootedness we need inside to cope with the frenzy around us.

※

The father was waiting with an answer when his somewhat lax 16-year-old son asked to be allowed to drive the family car. "Well, son," the father said, "if you go to church regularly, say your prayers, study your Bible and cut your hair, I'll think about it." About three months later, the boy asked again. "Well, son," the father said, "I admit you've certainly improved. You go to church weekly, you say your prayers regularly and you study your Bible consistently. But you still haven't cut your hair." "Well," the boy said, "I prayed for enlightenment about that, Dad, and it occurred to me that Abraham had long hair, Noah had long hair, Moses had long hair and even Jesus had long hair." "Yes," said the father, "and they walked everywhere they went." Beware prayer that sets out to accumulate but not to grow.

Naming

Isaiah 43:1

I have written your name on the palm of my hand.

"Sticks and stones may break my bones," we sang as children, "but names will never hurt me." I'm no longer sure of that—and I have two stories to prove it.

Years ago, when a man or woman made a public profession of religious vows, it was customary that they be given a new name to signify the taking on of a new existence, a new life. It was a kind of second baptism. I understand the situation very well. I was given the name "Mary Peter" in that long-ago world and disappeared behind it in a cloud of black serge. "Who are you?" the children in the playground loved to ask. "Who are you *really?*" The children had a point.

In fact, from the time of my having put on the name "Mary Peter" at the beginning of the novitiate, to the time of my putting it down almost fifteen years later to become who I really was again when an unwitting secretary assigned me by accident to a man's dormitory in a public university, the world changed. We laughed about the situation for years but it was more than funny. With the name change came a new understanding in me of what naming is really all about, what it implies, what it does and what it means—spiritually—to name something.

Monastic communities are given to naming. In our own monastery, for instance, we call one hall "Benedicta Riepp" in honor of the foundress of the Erie community. We call the other one "Scholastica Burkhard" in honor of our first prioress in 1856. We call the community bell "Theodore" in the custom of European monasteries who always named the carillon that called them to prayer. We give every sister a title— Sister Anne, of the Unfailing Generosity of God, for instance—to indicate some kind of patronage or quality of life that we see developing in them. We call the outdoor passageway that connects our two residence wings, and is lined with old community tombstones, the *Memento Morum*

Walkway (remember death) as a way of connecting the living members of the community with the deceased ones.

We give life to everything, in other words, by naming it. We make relationships even with things that are not present, are not human, by naming them. We invest life with meaning by naming the things around us that give us identity, direction and character. It is a tradition as old as the Old Testament itself. When Moses asks God, "What is your name?" God says, "I am who Am." After Jacob steals his brother's birthright and wrestles with the angel, God calls him "Israel," the one who has striven with God. Sarai becomes "Sarah," the one who laughed at the thought of being able to have children in old age.

Naming is clearly a holy act, an act of creation. It begets identity. But it can also destroy relationships. It's a powerful device that deserves to be used with caution, with reverence, with sacred trust.

❧

"The beginning of wisdom," the Chinese proverb teaches, "is to call things by their right names." Not by names we make up to trivialize them; not by names we use to deride them; not by names and titles we use to hide them from themselves but by their "right names." Think about the names you've been given in life. Are they your "right name"?

❧

Jews in the Nazi concentration camps had no names, only numbers tattooed on their arms. It was their first great death. There is no greater extinction than not to be called by name. What we do not address directly does not exist for us. And the people who are not being addressed know it.

❧

"The name we give to something," Katherine Paterson writes, "shapes our attitude toward it." Which, of course, is why children who grow up being called "Porky" or "Four Eyes" or "Crip" or "Junior" can come to resent those names so much. How much worse if you're called "nigger" or "spic" or "fag"—names of diminishment or ridicule—all your life.

❧

Calling someone by name is a mark of intimacy, of endearment, of acknowledgment. "Hey, you" is not a relationship.

❧

Last month, a woman in Britain cried as she talked about the loss of the family herd to foot-and-mouth disease. "I knew them each by name," she said. It brought into stark relief how easy it is to destroy what we do not bother to know, how difficult it is to hurt what we have bothered to know.

꙳

Naming gives a person identity and importance and uniqueness. To talk about "the girls" in data processing, "the doorman" in the building, "the guy" who picks up the garbage is to turn them into objects rather than people.

꙳

"Naming," Jessamyn West writes, "is a kind of caressing and fondling." There are people whom we love to have simply say our name. To be known to the core, to be cared about as a person is life's greatest aspiration.

꙳

What we name a thing says as much about us as it does about the thing we name. It signals the depth of understanding we have of what we name. It also signals the quality of the thought we bring to the process.

꙳

To refuse to learn to pronounce a person's name simply because its origin is different from our own is the supreme insult, the silent racism. No excuse is acceptable. "I just can't handle all those letters," "It's something 'ski'," "It's one of those names with all the syllables," "I'll just call you 'Strav,' OK?" are signs of disinterest, arrogance or ignorance.

꙳

A name gives historical and social quality. Or to put it another way: Try to think of Queen Elizabeth II as "Biffy" or George Washington as "Shorty." Be careful what you do to the human stature, your own or someone else's. In the final analysis, it's all we can give a person that really counts.

꙳

We used to name children after saints or great national figures. It gave them some kind of patronage, some kind of stature for which to strive. Now we name them after rappers and movie stars. What do you think that's saying? And is it about them—or about us?

❧

Naming labels a thing. And it can negate it, as well. At least that's what we did to the slaves in this country when we called them only by their first names. But when you take personhood, adulthood, maturity, visibility from someone by refusing to give them a name, you pay the price while they struggle to find it again.

❧

Naming is a holy act. It confers uniqueness on a person; it brings character into existence.

❧

Writers are very sensitive to the use of words. Ambrose Bierce, one of our greatest storytellers, wrote years ago what we have only begun to realize now. He said, "Miss: a title with which we brand unmarried women to indicate that they are in the market. Miss, Missis (Mrs.) and Mister (Mr.) are the three most distinctly disagreeable words in the language, in sound and sense. Two are corruptions of Mistress, the other of Master. . . . If we must have them, let us be consistent and give one to the unmarried man. I venture to suggest Mush, abbreviated to Mh." Point: What we call a thing creates it.

❧

Hubert Humphrey said, "Things are not only what they are. They are, in very important respects, what they seem to be." Or think of it this way: It's very hard to take "Boopsy" seriously, respectfully, whether she's a lawyer or not.

❧

Naming gives voice to the spirit in either a person or a thing. It reflects the touch of the creator.

❧

Naming is as much a curse as it is an act of creation. It yields blows from which a person may never recover. Martina Navratilova put it this way: "I came to live in a country I love; some people label me a defector. I have loved men and women in my life; I've been labeled 'the bisexual defector' in print. Want to know another secret? I'm even ambidextrous. I don't like labels. Just call me Martina."

❧

When we have to label everything we touch we may need to ask ourselves whether it isn't just possible that the tagging of others comes out of our own need to elevate ourselves by degrading everyone else.

❧

Thoreau wrote, "They who can pronounce my name aright, they can call me, and are entitled to my love and service." No relationship, no love. No identity, no response.

❧

Naming makes us part of something. We use family names to remember who we are and what we're expected to be on those days when we doubt our own inner and independent strength. Then we dig back into the family heritage and live up to it.

❧

We wear club logos. We name buildings and companies and restaurants and trees. And in the doing of those things admit that everything in the world has as much right to exist as we do.

❧

We name things in the community to keep our history alive in us, to remind us who and what we're supposed to be, to keep before our eyes always what we're responsible for stewarding through the ages.

❧

The proverb teaches that "a person with a bad name is already half-hanged." We have to be careful that we do not hang labels on people that make it impossible for them to become more than this one name implies.

❧

In scripture God brings the animals to the human for naming. In that simple act the human is brought to recognize the particular personality and worth of each living creature. Too bad we forget that so often.

❧

Naming has a great deal to do with war. What we name the enemy is what makes it possible to destroy them without thinking of them as people.

❧

Naming has a great deal to do with the identification of heroes. It might be an interesting party game to name the people to whom, as a nation, we raise statues or name buildings or hang portraits. The Germans do it for musicians. The Irish iconize their poets. And we?

❧

We name what we value and according to the value we give it. Think of the names you've been given. What do they say about you? About the persons who created them? About the relationship between you? Have they had a good or bad effect on you?

❧

A thing is for you whatever you call it. Don't say you're not prejudiced, not sexist, not racist and still insist on calling people what they themselves do not want to be called.

❧

"Do not fear . . . I have called you by name," Yahweh says to Isaiah. Once you understand the relational value of naming—or not—these become among the strongest words in scripture. The thought is overwhelming: Our God knows us. Our God has a personal relationship with each of us. Our God takes note of us. So much for a mechanistic world.

❧

To go through life naming everyone and everything gently, lovingly leaves a trail of godliness in its wake. Why? Because in the presence of one who calls them by name, no one feels rejected, left out, invisible or worthless. Because to give another human being a sense of value is to give the gift of life.

❧

When the man limped into the doctor's office, he was bent double, arms hanging, face contorted in pain. The woman across the waiting room looked at him as he struggled from the doorway to a seat and then inquired of him sympathetically, "Oh, dear. Arthritis with scoliosis?" "No," the man said back through gritted teeth. "Do-it-yourself with cinder blocks." See what I mean? You can't cure a thing until you can name the problem.

Ordinary Time

Psalm 145:2

Every day I will bless you, and praise your name forever and ever.

My father died when he was twenty-three and I was three. I inherited only one small thing from him for my small self. It was a palm-size prayer book that had one of those old-time prayer card poems in it, edged in black. I memorized it almost as soon as I could read. It said, *I have only just a minute / only sixty seconds in it / forced upon me / can't refuse it / didn't seek it / didn't choose it / but I will suffer if I lose it.* . . . As the years went by, the doggerel slipped from memory, the philosophy lost its allure. Then, I got older and discovered some things.

Time is the ground, the centerpiece, the glue and the glory of life. But it is not simple. The liturgical tradition has long divided time in two. There were, we learned as young novices, two kinds of days in life and two periods of the year. The days were either feast days or ferial days. The year was divided into "ordinary" time and . . . well, "extra-ordinary" time, I guess. This second segment of the year, come to think about it, I never heard anyone name at all. It was a number of times: Advent, Lent, the Christmas, Easter and Pentecost seasons.

That kind of information may be boring stuff but it's important stuff, too. Ordinary time, you see, was the longest period of all. It was the time when life went its long, dull way, predictable to the ultimate. Monday, the novices did the laundry; Tuesday, we did chapel, altar breads, and housecleaning; Wednesday, Thursday, Friday and Saturday we did it all again. More of the same. Same old, same old. Week after week, month after month, year after year.

Every once in a while, of course, life was punctuated by a feast day with its special meals and polyphonic liturgies but, in the end, the normal, the daily predominated. As it does for all of us yet. The commute, the paperwork, the housework, the school run, eat up day after day with mind-numbing regularity. And yet, it is in "ordinary" time that the really important things happen: our children grow up, our marriages and relationships grow older, our sense of life changes, our vision expands, our soul ripens.

No doubt about it, the prayer card was right: To lose the glory of ordinary time is to suffer the loss of the greater part of life.

❧

It's only what we learn while we're doing what seems to be basically routine that really counts: how to endure, how to produce, how to make life rich at its most mundane moments. "There are more truths in twenty-four hours," Raoul Vaneigem wrote, "than in all the philosophies."

❧

Only the ordinary makes the special, special. To be glutted with specialness is to lose all sense of the exceptional in life.

❧

The nice thing about repetition is that it gives us an opportunity to take a second look at everything around us before we miss what it is meant to teach us.

❧

Ordinary time is the mentor of us all. "A sub-clerk in the post office," Camus wrote, "is the equal of a conqueror if consciousness is common to them." Those who look at where they are and can see what they're looking at are those who make ordinary time extraordinary.

❧

To be considered "ordinary" has become an insult of sorts. But it is only the ordinary that has the ring of hard-won truth to it. Anything else is scam and whipped cream.

❧

The ordinary is what reveals to us, little by little, inch by inch, "the holiness of life, before which," Dag Hammarskjöld wrote, "we bow down in worship."

❧

Wait patiently for those interruptions of the ordinary that unmask for us the real core of the human condition: life, death, change.

❧

To be ordinary is not to be nondescript, bland, lifeless or wan. To be ordinary is to see the value of the daily without being cemented in it.

❧

It is important to understand the difference between stability and intransigence. Stability roots us in a past that, like good ground everywhere, nourishes what is growing. Intransigence roots us in a past that has been petrified in order not to have to grow at all.

❧

"The despotism of custom," the philosopher John Stuart Mill wrote, "is everywhere the standing hindrance to human advancement." Take it as a bad sign when you hear yourself arguing for something on the grounds that "we've always done it this way."

❧

"Everything passes, everything perishes, everything palls," the French say. There is nothing, in other words, in which the pulse of the ordinary does not beat. Hoping to live life on the edge all the time is not just adolescent, it is futile.

❧

We want life to be exciting, when as a matter of fact, life is only life. We want the spiritual to be mystical rather than real.

❧

Knowing that tomorrow will be much the same as today gives the kind of security a person needs to experiment with a little piece of it.

❧

Annie Dillard wrote, "How we spend our days is, of course, how we spend our lives." The tragedy is that we ignore so much of it in the interest of getting to the real stuff.

❧

Never confuse the ordinary with the simple, the static, or the boring. Living an ordinary life well can be a very complicated thing to do. It takes great talent to make a great life out of a routine one.

❧

"A cow must graze where it is tied," the Africans say. The little circumstances in which we find ourselves are the food of the soul. When I solve hunger problems in my hometown, I am healing a starving globe.

❧

To the real mystic, the passing of the seasons is never commonplace. It is the repetition that finally, finally opens our eyes to God where God has always been: right under the feet of us.

❧

Repetition is of the essence of monasticism. We repeat our daily schedule. In the first place, it frees the mind for greater thoughts. In the second place, it sensitizes the soul to the sacred poetry of the present moment. When the day is really routine we get to think awhile about what we're doing and why we're doing it and how we're doing it. It is the well from which we draw our reasons to go on.

❧

Simply staying where we are because there is nowhere else to go is not the answer. What makes the difference is to stay where we need to be with a sense of appreciation for dailiness. That is the real stuff of contemplation.

❧

The dailiness of spiritual practices, the practices of daily life, focus the heart and concentrate the mind. Incessant agitation, unending variety, constant novelty, a torrent of gadgetry, a life filled with the strange and the unfamiliar irritate the soul and fragment the inner vision.

❧

The desert monastics wove baskets every day of their lives to earn alms for the poor—and, when the baskets went unsold, unbraided them and began again. The purpose was to occupy the body and free the mind. Mindless work is not a burden when the mind is full and the heart like a laser beam finds its way to God.

❧

We run from place to place and thing to thing, we skirt from idea to idea and do not recognize God in the humdrum of the day-to-day.

❧

We wait for retreats, services, grand gatherings to take us to God, and God is with us all the while. We are just too preoccupied, too disassociated to notice.

❧

The routine parts of life, the dull parts of the day are the gifts of space. Then, while the world goes on around us, the thoughts of God take hold within us.

❧

If I cook dinner, that's ordinary. If I put a flower on the table when I serve it, that's divine.

❧

The function of routine is to give us time to recoup our energies for the next unpredictable challenge. Enjoy every minute of normal time you have. Store it in your heart as energy and endurance. You will someday need the peace and calm and certainty you have garnered there.

❧

"To live," Antoine de Saint-Exupéry wrote, "is to be slowly born." The fact is that coming to be fully alive is the task of a lifetime. There's so much in each of us that we have never touched, so much beauty we're steeped in that we've overlooked. Consciousness is what lifts the ordinary to the level of the sublime.

❧

Life, by definition, is warm and pulsating. Life, by definition, speaks of God. Unawareness of those things is not ordinary; it is pathological. Where is God in your life right now?

❧

I work at an ordinary desk; I live in an ordinary house; I drive a very ordinary car; I like ordinary food. The blessing of ordinariness is that it keeps me in touch with the rest of the human race and very, very interested in the extraordinary sacredness of the universe that is so unlike me, so inviting.

❧

We must remember to begin again, day after day, to turn dailiness into time with God.

COMMUNITY

Romans 12:5

*So we who are many are one body in Christ, and
individually we are members one of another.*

Years ago, in the 1950s and 60s, during what was later recognized as a post-war vocation boom, the young entered religious life in droves. Driven by years of global chaos and human horror, the spiritual nerve endings of the Western world were at their keenest. Newly aware of God's merciful deliverance and exhausted by the awareness of sin that comes in the wake of not just one, but two world wars, people turned to the spiritual life and a sense of dependence on God in record numbers. Churches were filled to overflowing, convents and monasteries doubled in numbers, institutional works thrived, religious life became the great nerve center of the church. What we did—the teaching, the nursing, the social welfare work—threatened to consume, to obliterate, what we were really meant to be: Christian communities called to be prophet to the church.

But community—commitment—is what life is really all about for everyone. Our own community entrance rituals are very clear about the fact that life is not lived alone. When a woman seeks admittance to the monastery, she is met in the foyer by the entire community. "What is it you seek?" the community asks. "To seek God with you," the woman answers. Later, when she becomes a novice, she's asked again what she seeks, called to the altar and given a copy of the Rule of Benedict under which she'll live this new life. If, a year later, she chooses to make temporary vows, she'll be called back to the altar again, marked by the community pin and bonded to the community which, by universal suffrage, has voted to accept her. Finally, three years later, if she chooses to remain in monastic life permanently, she will receive the fourteenth-century ring that is the sign of her perpetual profession while the entire community ratifies her total immersion in the group. The common energy, the group excitement, the historic flow is palpable in the chapel. The "alleluias" that are sung are not the song of the individual.

They are the thanksgiving of the group for a way of life stirred to newness again.

Membership in the monastery is clearly a joint endeavor, a mutual bonding, a common responsibility for one another, for mutual growth, and for the gospel. In a world built on rugged individualism, independence and self-sufficiency, it is a clear reminder that those things are neither the end nor the ideal. They are the sham that leaves us lonely at the end of every crowded day.

But the role of the group in individual development is not unique to monastic life. We all live life in a maypole of groups, each of them overlapping the others, all of them adding layers to our own identity as the years go by. We are really "members one of another." Membership shapes us. It marks us. It requires us to grow and to give and to leave the world a bit better than we found it.

❧

To belong to a community is to begin to be about more than myself.

❧

Belonging to something is the first step toward taking responsibility for the rest of the human community.

❧

Never forget that every group stands for something. To join one is not simply to socialize with friends; it is to commit oneself to advancing the goals of the community itself. To what groups do you belong and what is your presence there saying to the rest of the world?

❧

When we commit ourselves to the goals of a group, we get from the group as much as we give it. It requires us to listen, to learn, to live life in broader circles.

❧

People join groups in order to do together what cannot possibly be done equally as well alone. Choose your communities carefully. They are changing the world. More than that, they change you.

❧

"You are a member of the British royal family," Queen Mary said to her daughter Queen Elizabeth. "We are never tired and we all love hospitals." There are things we do in life because the groups to which we belong require that they be done by us or they may not be done at all.

❧

Commitment to a group has something to do with deciding what needs to be done and then setting out to do something, however small, to make it happen.

❧

Commitment and convenience are not synonyms. To really "belong" to something, I must do what the group is pledged to do whether I feel like it right now or not.

❧

The communities to which I belong are a measure of myself. They tell me what I care about, what I consider important, how I relate to the rest of humanity. Take an inventory of the groups to which you belong and you will learn a great deal about yourself that no psychologist can tell you.

❧

Everyone should belong to at least one group that is dedicated to the betterment of the human condition. What else gives us the right to complain that it hasn't happened, let alone hope that it will?

❧

Groups carry us when we cannot walk another step alone. They give us energy when our own runs dry. They are the reservoir of gifts that fills up all our weaknesses.

❧

The strength of a group is not determined by its numbers but by the intensity of its dedication to its goals. Every revolution on earth has been engineered by a small group, not by the masses.

❧

Only those who live beyond themselves ever become fully themselves.

❧

We need the group for our own spiritual advancement. In every holy group there are holy models, people who teach us how to live, how to fail, how to survive the blows of life.

❧

Never doubt the power of a group to focus the mind on ideas that transcend the daily and eclipse the mundane. They make us better than we know ourselves to be.

❧

The function of community is to bring us to greater self-knowledge, to expose our dark sides and call forth our strengths. Then, aware of our weaknesses but sure of our gifts, we spend our lives neither attempting too little nor trying to do too much.

❧

To become a serious member of a group is to allow others to know us, to lead us, to prod us to do more, to do better, to do something which, alone, we might never have either the courage or the conscious awareness to do.

❧

"To say 'yes,' you have to sweat and roll up your sleeves and plunge both hands into life," Jean Anouilh writes. Only when we're a contributing part, a risk-taking part, of something worth doing are we really committed. In fact, only then, perhaps, are we really alive.

❧

It's what we owe the rest of humanity that drives us into communities large enough to deal with large questions. None of us has the right to ignore what is eating the heart out of the world and call ourselves human.

❧

The nice thing about belonging to a good, healthy, committed community is that somebody's always feeling up when you're feeling down. That protects you from falling victim to your own pessimism.

❧

"There is no hope of joy," the writer Saint-Exupéry wrote, "except in human relations." No work is enough to satisfy the human soul. Only the satisfaction of having touched another life and been touched by one ourselves can possibly suffice. Whatever we do, however noble, however small, must be done for the sake of the other. Otherwise, we ourselves have no claim on the human race.

❧

"Responsibility," Winston Churchill wrote, "is the price of greatness." To be great we must be for the other. No one is great without the community that calls its greatness forth.

❧

Those who expect to be carried by others forget that to deserve it they must first do some carrying of their own.

❧

The whole notion of rugged individualism, self-sufficiency and independence is based on the myth of the autonomous self. The problem with that idea is that it takes a great deal of support to be autonomous.

❧

Every one of us has some gift to give, some reason to be alive, some part to play in the development of humanity. But if that is the case, then community has to be the coin of the realm. Otherwise, the gift is ungivable, the part is unplayable, the very purpose for which we were born has been forgotten.

❧

Community carries us over the rough spots of life. It lifts us in its current and moves us when we cannot move ourselves.

❧

And the scripture teaches, "Two are better than one because they have a good reward for their labor. For if they fall, the one will lift up their companion; but woe to those who are alone when they fall; for they have no one to lift them up" (Ecclesiastes 4:9–12). Beware self-sufficiency. It is a trap for the arrogant.

❧

The voice of the Holy Spirit is in the good heart of the other for us. Listen carefully and do not block out the messages of the group that is growing you.

❧

"Madam," Sydney Smith wrote, "I have been looking for a person who disliked gravy all my life; let us swear eternal friendship." It's the little things that bond us, that make us ready for the great ones, isn't it?

❧

No one becomes holy alone. Only constant, stable contact with others brings us the self-knowledge it takes to become what God wants us to be. No group, therefore, is unimportant to our own self-development.

❧

The wag wrote, "We the born naked, wet, and hungry. Then things get worse." And that, friends, is exactly why we need one another. It is in community that our nakedness is covered, our wetness dried, our hunger satisfied.

RITUALS

Psalm 95:6

*O come, let us worship and bow down,
let us kneel before God, our Maker.*

I remember the scenes as if they were yesterday. Every day after lunch, the novices corralled the postulants to teach us how to mark our breviaries in preparation for the afternoon Vespers. Part of the session included, too, how to perform the liturgical gestures that were part and parcel with daily prayer—and, come to think about it—part and parcel with every other part of the monastic life, as well. We even learned how to bow. A "simple bow"—head only—was reserved for the name of Jesus; a "moderate bow"—head and shoulders only—was used for references to the Godhead; a "profound bow"—head and shoulders bent waist deep, deep enough, that is, to enable a person to touch her knees in the process—was used at the end of every psalm in deference to the Trinity. We also bowed silently when we met another sister in a corridor. And when we passed a statue. In fact, we formalized a lot of life: we broke our bread into five pieces or three pieces at every meal and we said prayers as we dressed. Every action had a proper time or form or place. Every gesture was a sacramental.

The truth is that life long ago was one long panoply of gestures for most people. Children stood and said "Good morning, Sister" every time a nun entered the room. Men took off their hats when passing a church and women made the sign of the cross. Everybody genuflected when going into a church. Everybody took holy water when coming out. And almost nobody knew why. But they did know that those simple behaviors were a language of their own.

And now? Well, there's no doubt that things have changed. There's no doubt that we look back at some of the earlier practices with nostalgia as well as with a smile, perhaps. But gestures don't really die. We are gesture-making animals. When one set of gestures becomes obsolete, we create new ones. Like the formal presentation of gifts that is so often a part of the ritual of the Mass now. Or the handshake of peace. Or the emerging practice of lighting Advent candles to mark the weeks of preparation for Christmas. The question is, Why do we do these things, whatever they are? What's the purpose of gestures? Why not just go into church and sit down or stand up or do whatever we like wherever we like? The answers are too simple for words—as are the gestures themselves.

❧

Gestures are a simple language that transcends national barriers and even personal conversation. We don't have to say hello; we can just wave. We don't need to say we're sorry; we can simply strike our breasts. Gestures help us to communicate what we're feeling without having to say a word. They are the language of emotion.

❧

Ritual gestures not only express our feelings wordlessly but they form our feelings, as well. Years of kneeling down to pray can teach as much about the greatness of God as any amount of reading can do. Try it again, why don't you.

❧

Rituals bring the body in sync with the soul. They make the invisible visible. They put us consciously in the presence of God.

❧

It's one thing to sing "alleluia." It's another thing entirely to lift up our hands to the sky when we say it. One is an idea. The other is a feeling.

❧

Gestures are what enable us to experience what we're thinking about. We fill the sanctuaries of the monastery chapel with plants and candles—growth and energy—to remind ourselves that the center of our lives lies here.

❧

When we bring our bodies as well as our minds to prayer, we make the spiritual life as real as everything else we do. As real as our work, as real as our recreation, as real as the things we do for entertainment. Then, we make life whole.

❧

The spiritual life is nourished by very earthy things: by water, by light, by gesture, by bread and wine. Then we see the divine in the ordinary. And then, by virtue of the ordinary we find the divine everywhere.

❧

The only bridge between the human and the divine is the human. When we fail to put everything in life in the service of the sacred, we forever make a false separation of the two.

❧

Any gesture we do often enough—a hug, a smile, a genuflection—has the power to transform us. We become what we do.

❧

The rituals we do together make us a community, a family, an organization, a team. They bond us as companions on the way.

❧

At the end of every prayer period in a monastic community the prioress extends her hand and blesses the community. It is no idle gesture to realize day after day that God has been called down into the likes of us.

❧

The incense bearer surrounds the scripture, the altar and the community itself with sweet-smelling incense. The incense gives us an awareness of how rarified a space we create when each of us alone and together concentrates on the God among us. Without the incense to remind us, we might lose sight of the abiding presence of God, just as we lose sight of the air which we breathe.

❧

Gestures direct our minds. They concentrate us. They put thoughts in our head which we might otherwise never think of without them: humility, repentance, community, God.

❧

Rituals carry us through death and show us how to celebrate life. Without them we might get swept away by grief or forget to hallow those moments in life that are our rites of passage or milestones along the way.

❧

"Everything created by God," said the Baal Shem Tov, the reformer of Judaism, "contains a spark of holiness." The problem is that there's nothing easier to forget in life unless, of course, we mark it somehow. By sprinkling water on a casket, for instance, or by baptizing a newborn in a long white gown.

❧

To genuflect is to recognize the holiness that is everywhere around us.

❧

When we treat the ordinary with reverence, God becomes attainable here. When we manage to recognize God in the ordinary, it becomes sacred, too.

❧

"If you sanctify yourself, a little," the Talmud teaches, "you are sanctified a great deal." We do not become holy—immersed in God—all at once. We do it one simple gesture at a time.

❦

"Action is only coarsened thought," Henri-Frédéric Amiel wrote. Gestures, actions, movements are our attempt to say completely what words can only hint at.

❦

The truth is that people are creatures of action. Not to bring action—gestures, ritual, symbols—to our prayer life is to make it an intellectual rather than a human endeavor.

❦

Hang a crucifix or an icon in a special spot in your home. Every day, bow before it and light a small candle as sign of your awareness of the Spirit around you and see if you don't quickly become, not a person who prays, but a prayerful person.

❦

Friedrich Engels wrote once: "An ounce of action is worth a ton of theory." Don't say you love God when you never, ever go to a sacred spot to pray or regularly give yourself to some conscious, tangible embodiment of God's presence in your life. Action—gesture, ritual—is what connects us to the center of ourselves.

❦

What we do is what we are. Strange, isn't it, that we can fill our life with rituals that remove us from the humdrum—the Sunday golf game, the regular shopping trips, the Wednesday card club—but never realize that the spiritual life, too, must be fed by regular rituals or dry up and blow away like straw in the wind.

❦

"Never confuse movement with action," Ernest Hemingway wrote. Good ritual, real action must be done consciously.

We must know why we're doing what we're doing and what it says to us as well as what it says about us. The simple repetition of meaningless actions is not prayer, it's some kind of spiritual robotics.

❧

Ritual gestures center the soul and clear the mind and focus the heart.

❧

All the intellectualizing in the world cannot equal one single, lovely spiritual action. It does explain, however, how it is possible that people can study theology and not become holy.

❧

"Good actions ennoble us," Cervantes wrote, "and we are the children of our own deeds." What we do is what we will eventually become.

❧

Nobody "thinks" the spiritual life. They act it out. Both publicly and privately. But it is what we have trained ourselves to do privately that will eventually become the seed of the public self.

❧

"It is only when people begin to worship," Calvin Coolidge said, "that they begin to grow." Worship—the immersion in ritual gestures—is what leads us to grow into what we do. Then our souls become what our bodies desire.

❧

"Ritual is the way we carry the presence of the sacred," Christine Baldwin wrote. "Ritual is the spark that must not go out." When we cease to engage ourselves in ritual, we cease to connect the mundane with the sublime.

MUSIC

Psalm 150:3–6

Make music to bless God. Play lyre and harp. . . .
With resounding cymbals and drums,
let all sing praise to God.

I had wanted to be a sister for as long as I could remember. Long before I started school I knew where life would eventually lead. By the time I was in high school, I had begun the long and arduous process of community hunting. In those days, they had whole books devoted to descriptions of the various orders for a girl to browse through in study hall. It was a matter of choosing wimples from coifs and rosaries from neck crosses and black from brown, I thought. On one side of the page were a succession of smiling young nuns in long dark dresses, all of them basically alike, all of them clearly different. On the other side of the page was a commentary on the history and ministries of each group, complete with mailing addresses through which the ardent could get additional information. It worked. I wrote to Maryknoll. I wrote to a group of Carmelites. I wrote to the cloistered Benedictines at Clyde, Missouri. It was a toss-up: mission work around the world or a small cloister somewhere off the beaten track.

Then, one night, just as I was leaving the high school grounds, I became conscious of the sound of the chant coming out of the second-floor chapel windows as I never had heard it before. It was pure as spun steel, high and rhythmic and unending. It swirled through the yard and caught me up in itself and put me down on the other side of my decision. It was obvious; the music was the answer. Somewhere deep inside me I knew what I had known all the time: In the end, I would follow the music.

I'd been playing the piano for ten years. When nothing else calmed me or stirred my soul, music did. To this day, I am fond of telling people who ask me what my day is like that I live life between two keyboards. The one, my computer, sits at one end of my desk and empties my soul. The other, my keyboard, sits at the other end of the desk, and when the day is too long or the empty page too daunting, fills it up again. No doubt about it: Music brought me to the monastery as surely as any description of the community's ministries did.

Benedictine monasteries live on music. They sing psalms and hymns and the readings of the church. They sing all the time. Benedictine life is immersed in music. Why? Because the Benedictine knows, as did the psalmist musician-poet thousands of years ago, that God speaks the unspeakable in music. And what else is life about if not an endless attempt to discover the unspoken?

❧

Music slakes the thirst for beauty. It comes on us out of nowhere and touches something in us that we never knew we had.

❧

"Music touches places beyond our touching," Keith Bosley wrote. The Jewish community, a people without a place for thousands of years, gave very expressive music the honored site in their hearts and in their prayer. Music was the one art that could be carried with them without burden in their flight from one refuge to another. Home, we learn from them, is as much the music of feeling as it is a place.

❧

Music is the sound of the universal soul crying out the pain and hope and faith that all our private little exiles bring to life in us. "Where there's music," Cervantes wrote, "there can be no evil." Or, at very least, the evil can be purged by beauty.

❧

All music is music, some of it more primitive, some more educated and cultivated and complex, yes, but all of it as natural, as telling, as the cry of the newborn in glee, in hope, in distress. The spiritual task is to determine what is being said in Mozart that is different from what is being said in rap.

❧

Music is the poetry of the poor, the traveler, the empty-handed.

❧

The symphony makes life, mundane and bare, a symphony of its own.

❧

Some music exalts the human spirit and demonstrates the acuity of the human mind. Some music reduces a love for rhythm and the joy of melody to the banal. It comes without depth, without gentleness and adds only to the world's store of the raucous and the vulgar. Beware the differences. Your soul may be at stake.

❧

"Jazz came to America 300 years ago," Paul Whiteman said, "in chains." The soul that is full of music is full of a wealth and a freedom of expression that no one can enslave.

❧

Music is the only language that transcends the boundaries between the ultimacy of God and the incapacity of humans. "I haven't understood a bar of music in my life," Igor Stravinsky, the great composer, wrote, "but I have felt it."

❧

Music does not "mean"; it expresses. Prayers that can't be formulated in prose are always best sung.

❧

Words grow old and predictable, even in prayer. But music with its twists and turns, harmonies and dissonance, lifts us always out of where we wish we were at any given moment to struggle with where we are. It touches into the emotional realities of the self that we would often like to avoid.

❧

So afraid were we of feelings at one point in human history that even music began to be hemmed in by rules and constraints and controls. But always and everywhere, sooner or later, a march, a Christmas carol, a great organ postlude, a broken-hearted hymn on Good Friday burst through, thank God, to make us human again.

❧

Music is the one thing from which we cannot hide our souls. It worms its way into our hearts and wrenches them open to the now.

❧

The dips and swells of plain chant turn prayer into an encounter with the holy that waits just beyond the edges of the words.

❧

To dance a prayer is to abandon ourselves to the God of the wind and the rain where grace pours out wild and free.

❧

Music is a reminder of the mystery of God. A hopeful reminder that the mystery is gracious.

❧

There is music in the cosmos, music in the sea, music in the wind, music untrammeled and untrapped in the human heart. Releasing it within ourselves is a first step on the way to a soaring spiritual life.

❧

The Scottish proverb reads: "Twelve Highlanders and a bagpipe make a rebellion." We do a lot of things to music we would never do without it: like hope and smile and try harder and explode into feeling down to the quiver in our knees.

❧

Music—national anthems, theme songs, hymns, barbershop quartets—binds a people. "Who hears music," Robert

Browning wrote, "feels his solitude peopled at once." Unless we have a group music, we don't have a group. In fact, we don't even have a self.

༚

The music pieces we love are the memories we cherish. They are the family, the spiritual life, the dreams of our lives.

༚

If you know what music it is that you can't bear to hear, you'll know what memory it is that you haven't come to peace with yet.

༚

When God put music into the human heart, God put prayer there. Real prayer, not recitations of the formulaic.

༚

"Of all musical instruments," Shusha Guppy wrote, "the human voice is the most beautiful, for it was made by God." Clearly God wants us to do more with our voices than simply complain, report, praise and plead. God wants us to let loose.

༚

The reason we don't dance as much as the human spirit deserves is because we don't trust our bodies, we don't trust our feelings, we don't trust our truth. So we hem it in and pen it up and wonder why we have ulcers and esophagitis.

༚

Music takes us beyond knowledge to insight. We understand what we could not possibly understand otherwise. Knowledge is limited. Understanding is boundless. Everyone in a Benedictine community sings, not because they're singers but because singing releases the part of us that needs to be in tune with God.

❧

Everyone is musical. That comes with the body. Not everyone is a musician. When we confuse the two we leave a part of our deepest selves untapped. Put on the CD, turn it up, let go. When it's over, you'll be a different person. A freer one. Maybe even a better one.

❧

The church that does not sing is a church in which prayer and liturgy have been reduced to one part performance, three parts magic—where one person does it for everyone and we hope it works its way into the deepest part of our souls and makes the necessary changes we need there.

❧

My Benedictine community is a singing community. Maybe that's why we're a community at all, come to think about it. Amiel puts it this way: "Music is harmony, harmony is perfection, perfection is our dream, and our dream is heaven."

❧

Music is good for nothing except for making something out of our mundane souls.

❧

Despite all this, I have a friend who says she wouldn't know middle C if she fell over it, and there are lots of Benedictines who are tone deaf, too, I bet. Point: Music works as well in the shower as it does anywhere else. And anyway, as Beecham said, "Composers should write tunes that chauffeurs and errand boys can whistle."

TABLE FELLOWSHIP

Wisdom 16:20

You nourished your people with food of angels and furnished them bread from heaven.

When you're a novice you begin to notice the little things: how a novice mistress pulls at her veil when she's amused, for instance; or how she pulls on her scapular when she isn't; how the sister in the wardrobe stands with her arms spread on the countertop if she's not too busy to be bothered; how the portress's tone of voice changes when you ask her to page a person for the fourth time in a row. What our novices noticed was that there were always raisins in the oatmeal on "speaking days," feast days great enough, that is, to justify the community's talking at meals.

There were eleven "speaking days" on the community calendar in those days, not enough to bother memorizing the list, but enough to warrant keeping your eyes on the oatmeal. "What if," the novices assigned to kitchen duty wondered, "you put raisins in the oatmeal on *feria* or ordinary days? Would the prioress think it was a feast day and automatically say the prayer that signaled permission to speak at breakfast?"

So one day they tried it. Mother Sylvester looked at her oatmeal, looked up at her council sitting nearby, looked back down at the oatmeal, pushed a raisin or two to the side of the bowl to inspect them more closely, looked up at the community, frowned a little frown, stared at the raisins—and gave the praise.

I remember the happy buzz of excitement in the dining room, the confusion at the head table as prioress and council checked their *ordos* and their pocket calendars, the giggle at the novices' table—and the look of horror on the novice mistress's face. I also remember that it never happened again. But the point had been made: Feast days have something to do with food. The celebration of life has something to do with food. Food is the glue and the center of human community making.

I began to understand life and community and celebration and Eucharist a great deal better.

❧

To share a meal with another person is the beginning of understanding. Breakfast meetings and business lunches are a contradiction in terms. We meet and do business or we eat and we talk. We don't do both at the same time because one is official and one is personal. Never the twain shall meet.

❧

It's at a meal where all of life comes together: talk, time, beauty, rest, and our awareness of our fascination with people and our need for one another.

❧

Mealtime is a microcosm of all life: there are few other times in the day when the interdependence of a group is more palpable. Here we prepare food for one another, serve it, share it, clean it up and do the dishes together. Here everyone is equally responsible for everyone else. When one person is expected to serve everyone else all the time, on all occasions, that's not family, that's servitude.

❧

"A guest in the house," a Russian proverb says, "is a feast for the family." To celebrate with food is to give what you have to others but it is also to enjoy what you have been given yourself. It is a sign that we are able to give of ourselves to care overflowing and joy without limits.

❧

Food connects us to nature, to ourselves, to the future. It must never be taken lightly. Everything we eat is either developing us or destroying us. When we choose what we eat, it is an act of creation second only to the conception of life.

❧

"To the one with an empty stomach," Gandhi says, "food is god." To lack food is to narrow life to the most primitive of agendas. How can a person enjoy beauty, concentrate on beauty, create beauty, think beautiful thoughts when what they're worrying about is what, if anything, they will have to eat next? And we wonder why the poor sections of a city are so drab, so uncared for.

❧

In my community, as in any family, it's at the table that we get to know each other. We discover what the day was like for the sisters around us, we hear what we believe as individuals about the world around us, and as older and younger sisters mix, we teach ourselves what our history is as a group. What do you talk about at table? The complaints of the day or the joys of the day?

❧

"A good meal," the French say, "ought always to begin with hunger." Nothing takes the joy out of eating like overeating.

❧

Constant snacking is a habit that breaks down a person's real appreciation for food. When we eat all the time, we aren't eating at all. We're simply feeding our irritations and reducing our consciousness of re-creation.

❧

Modern culture has turned food into an obsession: All we think about is what we should or shouldn't eat. It's hard to tell which one is worse.

❧

If you can have a meal with an enemy, you won't be enemies much longer. How is it possible to share the goods of the earth with someone and hate them at the same time? Tip: When you're uncertain about whether or not you like someone, invite them to have a meal with you and odds are that you will.

❧

To prepare a meal for someone is to give of yourself in ways that you know will please the other. That's why cooking is not a female thing. The very thought of engendering the act of family cooking makes us look again at the very concept of family.

❧

There are days of the year when we eat special meals, with special menus or special desserts. Thanksgiving and Christmas and Easter and ethnic picnics and birthdays all have special foods attached to them. For me it was watermelon on the Fourth of July because that's how my stepfather courted me while he was courting my mother. Years after he died, I still eat watermelon every Fourth of July. Food connects us with people—even when they're not here.

❧

The purpose of repeating menus long after the initial event is over is not the food at all. It is the bank of memories and associations that the food brings with it. So, in a way, thanks to the food, the event never dies. You have to wonder if life without special foods is really life at all.

❧

"Food should not be a merchandise to be bought and sold as jewels are bought and sold by those who have the

money to buy," Pearl Buck wrote. "Food is a human neces-
sity, like water and air, and it should be available." Of all the
things that should not be "reformed" as a country reforms its
welfare programs, surely it is food stamps. Maybe that's why
Jesus came as "the bread of life."

❧

A meal is a social act. It bonds people. "Sadder than des-
titution, sadder than a beggar," Jean Baudrillard says, "is the
one who eats alone in public."

❧

If you want to make a neighborhood, throw a neighborhood party: hot dogs in the backyard, pizza on the apartment
building roof. Serve anything anywhere but serve it to everyone and watch the social climate of a strange place change.

❧

When we were novices, we were not permitted to eat between meals. I found that very strange. After all, what's
wrong with having an apple between times? But as I got older
I began to realize that food is too special to be taken that
lightly.

❧

"Gluttony," Peter De Vries wrote, "is an emotional escape, a sign that something is eating us." If we have to quiet
our anxieties by eating, if we find that we are eating, not because we're hungry but to make ourselves feel good or to give
us permission to rest a while, it's clear that we really ought to
be dealing with what's bothering us in the first place.

❧

There is pain that comes from having too little food,
comfort in having special foods and a kind of silent self-
destruction in eating too much food.

❧

To share food with a person is to share life with them. It is a very meaningful act that deserves concentrated time, artistic presentation and thoughtful preparation. Animals eat; people dine.

❧

Throwing food on a table for quick consumption and basic survival reduces its spiritual meaning, its social value and its human dimension. It makes eating more an act of husbandry rather than an act of communion with the earth and a song of celebration of life.

❧

The fact that we have turned our world into one large fast food drive-in or cafeteria line may be part of the reason that we have become such an alienated culture. We never sit down long enough with anybody to get to know them, not even our families or our neighbors or our coworkers or our children.

❧

Learning to cook well, to serve beautiful dinners on well-set tables, to make a meal a sacrament of human community is the first step on the road to learning the art of life.

❧

The wag wrote, "We used to say 'What's cooking?' when we came home from work; now we say 'What's thawing?'" The question is, What has happened to a life that is too busy to cook a meal, too busy to put it on plates on a table to serve it, too busy to sit down to eat it? And is that busyness or is that suicide . . . of one kind or another?

❧

Mourn the loss of the daily family meal. Judith Martin may have said it best: "The dinner table is the center for the teaching and practicing not just of table manners but of conversation, consideration, tolerance, family feeling, and just about all the other accomplishments of polite society except the minuet."

❧

Never argue at mealtime. In the first place, it gives people ulcers. In the second place, it insults the cook.

❧

A Latvian proverb teaches that "A smiling face is half the meal." Go to a meal to enjoy the company and the food will take care of itself.

❧

To use food as a political weapon may be the greatest social sin of them all. Or, as Senator George Aiken put it, "I've never known a country to be starved into democracy."

❧

"Too much food spoils the appetite," the Chinese proverb says, "and too much talk becomes worthless." If you want to enjoy a good meal, eat a little less. If you want to enjoy a conversation, listen more.

❧

And then there's the line in the church bulletin that read (no kidding): "Pot luck supper in church basement. Prayer and medication to follow." Now there's a crowd that simply doesn't get it.

THE MYSTERY OF DEATH

Psalm 23:4

*Even though I walk through the darkest valley,
I fear no evil; for you are with me; your rod and
your staff comfort me.*

When two young sisters of ours, Sister Mary Bernard with whom I had taught, and Sister Ellen with whom I had entered the community, were killed along with their parents in an auto accident, the gaping vacuum they left in our midst plunged the entire community into a dull and distant numbness of soul. We had all lost sisters; I had lost a longtime friend. A kind of automatic faith there was aplenty, of course, but smiles were hard won and real hearty laughter seemed gone forever. Then, one letter came during that period that had a different ring to it.

The writer was one of the great women of the Benedictine Order. She had been a prioress for years, a director of novices, a national leader. She was, we all knew, a deeply spiritual woman. Not a pious one, a real one. She was, as well, a quiet, thoughtful woman, the kind of listener who never said much in a conversation, but this letter of hers was fulsome and to the point. To this day, I remember only one line of it, but that one line changed the way I looked at a lot of things ever after. "Death deprives," she wrote to me, "but it also enriches. You may not realize that now but you will come to see the truth of it sooner than you think."

It's thirty years later and the words become clearer every day. In the first place, after Ellen and Bernard died, we all became more precious to one another than we had been before. All these years later, as I watch the community meet the body of a sister at the door of the monastery, a regular part of our funeral rituals, I know that the community grows as much stronger with the death of each of us as it does at the entrance ceremony of someone new to the group. When I hear the prayers for the dying going on in the hall outside the death room and the monastery bell calling us all to the bedside of someone we've lived with and learned from and loved for years, I know that we are all richer in our grief for having been ministered to by this woman.

As I pass the necrology board outside of chapel, the list of all the deceased members of the community since 1856, I realize that no one ever dies in this community, they simply stay with us differently. As I cross from one side of the monastery to the other, through the Garden of Memories and under the *Memento Morum* Walkway (remember death), the pillars of which are inset with the tombstones of the sisters whose lives bought this property, built this building, and trained generation after generation of young nuns after them, I know that we haven't really lost them. They simply live now in other ways in us. It's true, I think, over and over again, "Death deprives but it also enriches." It makes us more reflective, more grateful for life, more aware of our debts to humanity, more conscious of the meaning of our own lives. Death is a very vibrant thing. It makes us all begin together again, more grateful for one another than ever before.

❧

Death launches a person into new orbits. It makes us find our way alone again. It requires us to start over. It grows us in ways we never would have chosen but dearly need to learn.

❧

Death is not difficult because it ends a relationship. Death is difficult because it ends the memory-making that is the real substance of life. "There is no greater grief," Dante wrote, "than the misery of recalling happier times."

❧

Memories give emotional substance to life. Without our memories we have only our biological selves and our work with which to identify. To live well we must never reject the opportunity to know another person well enough to miss their going.

❧

"The body dies," the Dhammapada says, "but the spirit is not entombed." The spirit of a person is what lives on in the people who loved them long after the body has done its work.

❧

When a sister dies, the community gathers the night before the funeral mass for the "Celebration of Memories" service. We tell one another the stories of that sister's presence in our individual lives. Some might call the gathering a waste of time. But we know that there is a value to taking an emotional inventory every once in awhile. Knowing that something of everyone we've ever known lives on in our own lives is to realize how gifting the world has really been to us.

❧

Just as the fetus resists birth, so does each of us resist death. Strange. If life has any meaning at all, then death is

just as certainly as much the birth canal to new and better being as is the birthing process to a fresh and challenging life.
But, oh, like the fetus, how we cling to the warm, the dark
and the familiar.

❧

"That day, which you fear as being the end of all things,"
the Roman Seneca wrote, "is the birthday of your eternity."
Since thanks to a good God things have been so good so far,
why is it that we doubt that they will be even better to come?

❧

Since dying is a natural part of life, what can possibly be
wrong with it? "The act of dying," Marcus Aurelius wrote, "is
also one of the acts of life." Hiding it, denying it, resisting it
only refuses it the gifts of spiritual anticipation and faith and
preparation that it offers.

❧

God allows death to give us all a regular opportunity to
reflect on what we're doing with our life.

❧

When we give up on anything worth doing, we stamp
out possible new life in ourselves and condemn ourselves to
die over and over again.

❧

It is not death that defeats us. It is refusing to live all the
life we have that deadens the heart and the soul even as it
beats, even while it breathes.

❧

The question is not whether you can talk to the people
you love after they die. The question is whether or not you
stopped long enough to listen to them while they were alive.

❧

There's a time in life when we start reading the obituaries before we read the headlines of the daily paper. That's the sign that we have finally figured out how precious life really is. If it hasn't happened to you yet, pray God it will.

❧

"Death," according to the Tibetan Book of Living and Dying, "is a mirror in which the entire meaning of life is reflected." Ask yourself now for what you want to be remembered and you will know exactly how you want to live the rest of your life.

❧

To lament the life of someone we've lost is the greatest tribute one human being can pay to another. Have you met the person whose loss you'll grieve yet? And if not, it may be time to ask what that's saying about your own ability to relate to life.

❧

No one can prepare for death. We can only live life in such a way that every night there's something for which to be grateful and every morning there is something for which to get up.

❧

Death is God's way of leading us to respect life. As long as the environment is destroyed with impunity and children are beaten unmercifully and people are starved without national remorse, the lessons of death have yet to be learned.

❧

Every death we live through is meant to teach us something. Allowing ourselves to deal with that consciously is important because every death around us brings us one step closer to our own.

❧

Death is a promise as well as a threat. It is the only re-minder we have that whatever it is that is bothering us now will, indeed, someday finally end.

❧

Death is the great mystery of life. It fascinates us. It is life's greatest surprise. If we hadn't been made to fear it so much, we would look forward to death giggling, like children at the great Christmas tree of life.

❧

We cling to life as if, in the face of the universe, it was God's only good. And yet, think about it, we certainly didn't miss it till we had it. So, what's the problem now? Or as the Roman Lucan put it, "The gods conceal from us the happi-ness of death, that we may endure life."

❧

We resent death as if we were the architects of our own lives and had a right to them. Joyce Cary put it this way: "I look upon life as a gift from God. I did nothing to earn it. Now that the time is coming to give it back, I have no right to complain."

❧

The person who is always waiting for a better time to do something is already largely dead.

❧

When we have loved someone enough to consider the world empty once they depart it, we have finally come to life ourselves.

❦

We measure the worth of a person after their death but we exercise the worth of them while they live. A raw courage for life is the dimension by which we calibrate the distance between the two.

❦

Death does not release us from life—it releases us from ourselves so that we can enjoy what life tries to give us.

❦

There is a death of spirit that is far worse than the death of the body. It drains us of energy and care and commitment. It drags us down until we determine for ourselves to rise up and begin again.

❦

Every person who dies demands that someone else live differently. Death is the invitation to those of us who are left behind to do what we have never done before, to do it confidently and to do it joyfully so that we do not die before we have allowed ourselves to live fully.

❦

Death is a moment of enlightenment. It is that pause in life that gives us the right to double over with pain, without apology, without embarrassment. It is the moment God uses to remind us that we alone, not someone else, are responsible for our happiness, our attitudes, our development, our failings. The truth is that death throws us back on ourselves. No wonder we cry so hard.

❦

The chaplain of the local chapter of Gamblers Anonymous prayed solemnly for those who had died since the last meeting of the group. "Our brothers have not died; they only sleep," the chaplain intoned over and over again. Finally, a guy in the back of the hall yelled out, "OK, pastor, you bet your way, I'll bet mine. Here's fifty to one says they're dead."

WAITING

Isaiah 9:1

The people who walked in darkness
have seen a great light.

Waiting has become a public occupation for us all. We wait for phones to ring and lines at checkout counters to shrink and classes to be over. We wait for the baby to go to sleep and for a granddaughter to stop by. We wait for the social security check to come and for the neighbors to turn off the boom box so we can finally think a bit. We wait for the mail carrier to come and the paper to arrive and the news to come on. I spend my life waiting for planes to take off and for computers to come on and for printers to print. They are all mundane things. But as a result, waiting is a both a social disease and a grace in our lives. The trouble is that we have to choose between them. The trouble is that we spend life waiting without knowing how to wait.

But not in my monastery. Here we are good at waiting. In fact, we liturgize it. Advent—the four-week waiting period that leads up to Christmas—is a series of events designed not to delay the celebration of Christmas, but to enhance it. It's a kind of delayed gratification that culminates in a kind of satisfaction that is all the richer for the waiting.

We hold weekly Advent vigils where prayer in the candlelit dark is a metaphor for life in general. We light hanging vigil candles down the hallway to chapel a little at a time to light the path to the spiritual center of the monastery. We watch the lights on the huge Advent wreath in chapel brighten from week to week. We don't play Christmas carols before Christmas. We don't hang decorations until Christmas week itself. We wait—and we prepare inwardly as we go.

And then suddenly, Christmas blazes everywhere: the O Antiphons sing of desire for the fullness of the spiritual life, crèches from around the world begin to emerge in every corner of every hall, the Christmas crib is blessed by the community, the tree is decorated and lit, the choir sings international carols and the waiting for new life becomes the thing itself. Contemplative waiting, purposeful waiting is what makes Christmas an experience rather than simply an event. It is a lesson meant to color the entire year.

❧

We can wait empty or we can wait full. It all depends on what we do with the time. Those who wait empty get irritated or dissipated. Those who wait full get richer as the time goes by.

❧

Those who wait empty wait aimlessly. Those who wait full do something that changes even themselves by the time they get what they are waiting for.

❧

Christmas is not meant to be an orgy of getting. It is meant to be the contemplation of the possibility of new life—even in ourselves.

❧

Advent enables us to consider again what it is about the spiritual life that is trying to be born in us again: a new desire for God, the hope in God's goodness, the signs of God around us that we so often overlook, the awareness of God in strange places. Without Advent, we run the risk of missing Christmas, too.

❧

Without the grace of anticipation, no experience could ever be sweet to the full.

❧

"Nothing we wait for," La Rochefoucauld wrote, "ever thoroughly answers our expectations but it does, then, leave us something to desire." And having something to desire is always a Christmas for the heart.

❧

"What we anticipate seldom occurs," Disraeli wrote, and "what we least expected generally happens." Preparation is the process of being ready for both.

❧

The important thing is to stay in the waiting itself, to concentrate on internal preparation for important moments more than on the external trappings that go with them. Otherwise we will become so immersed in our fantasy of them that we will never really be ready for the thing itself.

❧

We put away Thanksgiving on Thursday and leap into Christmas on Friday as if the in-between time had no value except for shopping and running from one set of parties to another. Then we wonder why our hearts aren't in it when we've done nothing to prepare our hearts for all of it in the first place.

❧

The nice thing about waiting is that it is good for the soul. "We love to expect," Samuel Johnson wrote, "and when expectation is either disappointed or gratified, we want to be again expecting." Expectation is the great spiritual snare of life. It tells us always that there is more to life than we now know. It leads directly to God.

❧

Waiting is an education in the self. It tells us who we really are and how we really go about the great adventure of life: thoughtfully, hurriedly, greedily, deeply.

❧

Waiting is what saves us from becoming slaves to the future. It enables us to think of options in case what we wait for fails to come. It requires that we fill the time in ways that swell the spirit. It gives us a sense of the present.

❧

It isn't waiting that is a problem. It's how we wait that determines the quality of our lives, both spiritual and psychological.

❧

The capacity to wait is the ability to endure, to grow, to enjoy and to hope.

❧

Waiting is that dimension of hope that enables a person to prepare without guarantee of fulfillment.

❧

To rush from one major event to another without having the opportunity to savor the days in between them simply dulls the relish for the thing itself. It isn't food that delights us; it's the way it's prepared that makes the difference. It isn't the event that changes us; it's the character of the waiting.

❧

Advent, if we really attend to it, is the feast of life. It reminds us that the journey to newness is long and dark and may in the end still look as if it has not arrived. Then we may know at last that we have come to that sense of emptiness which only God can fill.

❧

Advent is a search in the dark. It is "a call to live wide awake," Philip Berrigan and Elizabeth McAlister wrote, "so that we can be alert to God working in us." It is the call to tend again whatever lights may be dying in our own hearts and to wait for them to be enkindled however they can.

❧

Advent sets us on a road to new insight, new awareness and new spiritual energy.

❧

Learning to wait well is one of the secret gifts of the soul. It gives growing time in the dark.

❧

Waiting is not a passive thing. It takes character. It takes a commitment to prepare beyond the superficial so that an event can have significance as well as celebration.

❧

To celebrate Christmas well, it is necessary to live Advent well. Learning to wait in holy anticipation is part of the spiritual exercise of life.

❧

The basic message of Advent is that hope never dies: not our hope in God or God's hope in us.

❧

The lack of contemplative consideration that comes with Christmas consumerism too often drowns out the sounds of Advent. What's worse, it not only drains the meaning out of Christmas but even, perhaps, the rest of the year as well.

❧

Christmas does not only commemorate the birth of Jesus. It is really meant to mark our own new beginning of spirit and life and understanding and commitment for which we have waited all our lives.

❧

Thanks to Advent we know now that delight in life is an attribute of God crying to be developed in us.

❧

If it weren't for Advent we might miss the message that we are not called to be perfect; we are only called to be sorry. So we can go on going on. Otherwise the search for the unattainable might smother search in us completely.

❧

Christmas is proof that powerlessness is not weakness. On the contrary, it is a call to courage.

❧

B. C. Forbes wrote, "Anything that inspires unselfishness makes for our ennoblement." Christmas measures our unselfishness quotient.

❧

Be grateful for what is ending. Prepare for what is ahead by readying the soil of the soul for anything and everything God sends.

❧

"May you have the greatest two gifts of all on these holidays," John Sinor wrote. "Someone to love and someone who loves you." And that, dear friends, is in the end what happy new years are made of.